Wreck of the Red Arrow

By Richard Clark

INFINITY
PUBLISHING.COM

Copyright © 2009 by Richard Clark

ISBN 0-7414-5381-9

Published by:

INFI∞ITY
PUBLISHING.COM

1094 New DeHaven Street, Suite 100
West Conshohocken, PA 19428-2713
Info@buybooksontheweb.com
www.buybooksontheweb.com
Toll-free (877) BUY BOOK
Local Phone (610) 941-9999
Fax (610) 941-9959

Printed in the United States of America
Published August 2009

An upper berth is exchanged for a lower berth. A young man races to catch a train that is quickly leaving the station. A father surprises his family by joining them on the last leg of their trip. Mundane events to be sure, important only to the people involved. But in a few hours, nothing will be the same; up will be down, down will be up. People and their possessions will be strewn about a remote hillside in Pennsylvania. The Pullman cars they were riding and sleeping in will be smashed and scattered like sticks in the wind. All this is taking place on a cold night on February 18, 1947 around 3:21 a.m. near the town of Gallitzin.

The crack Pennsylvania Railroad passenger train 'RED ARROW,' hauling a normal load of fourteen Pullman cars, left Detroit's Fort Street Union Depot Station at 5:20 p.m. on Monday. Destination: Penn Station in New York City. Estimated time of arrival: 8:50 a.m. the next day.

But it never made it. Coming out of the tunnel at Gallitzin at a high rate of speed, it was unable to hold the track rounding Bennington Curve, 1.18 miles away, and derailed. This resulted in the first Pullman cars plus the two K4 engines, with their tenders, tumbling and skidding down the steep slopes of Gum Tree Hollow more than 200 feet below.

Detroit's Fort Street Station with its four tower clocks, each 10 feet in diameter, was used by the Pennsylvania Railroad until 1959. The Station was closed in 1971 and demolished in 1974 despite efforts to save it.

The last four cars (11, 12, 13, and 14) remained upright and on the tracks. Some Pullman cars made it all the way to the bottom of the hollow and were badly damaged.

The Pennsylvania Railroad main line at this junction consisted of four tracks:

Track No. 1 was for eastbound freight.

Track No. 2 was for eastbound passengers.

Track No. 3 was for westbound freight.

Track No. 4 was for westbound passengers.

All four tracks run parallel to each other.

The rails of Bennington Curve can be seen in this photo, like the iceberg waiting for the Titanic. To the left is the downward slope of Gum Tree Hollow.

This photo is one of twenty-four that were left undeveloped in a camera for thirty years. The name of the photographer is not known.

The Red Arrow was using track No. 2, the third track in from the steep slopes of Gum Tree Hollow. As track No. 2 exits the east portal of the Gallitzin tunnel, it bears to the left.

It straightens out for a short distance as it descends in elevation. This is followed by a sharp turn to the right, which is where the derailment occurred. This is Bennington Curve, 1.18 miles from the east portal of the Gallitzin tunnel. Horseshoe Curve is four miles farther down these same tracks, and the city of Altoona is just beyond that. When the train started to derail, instead of having flat open ground to fall on, it had the descending slope of Gum Tree Hollow to contend with. Had the terrain been flat, less damage would have occurred and fewer lives would have been lost. The point of derailment was at the worst possible spot.

Engine No. 422 (Lead Engine)

Fabricated in East Altoona

10-23-38

Lead Engineer Mike Billig in front of K4 Engine No. 5408

This engine was not involved in the wreck

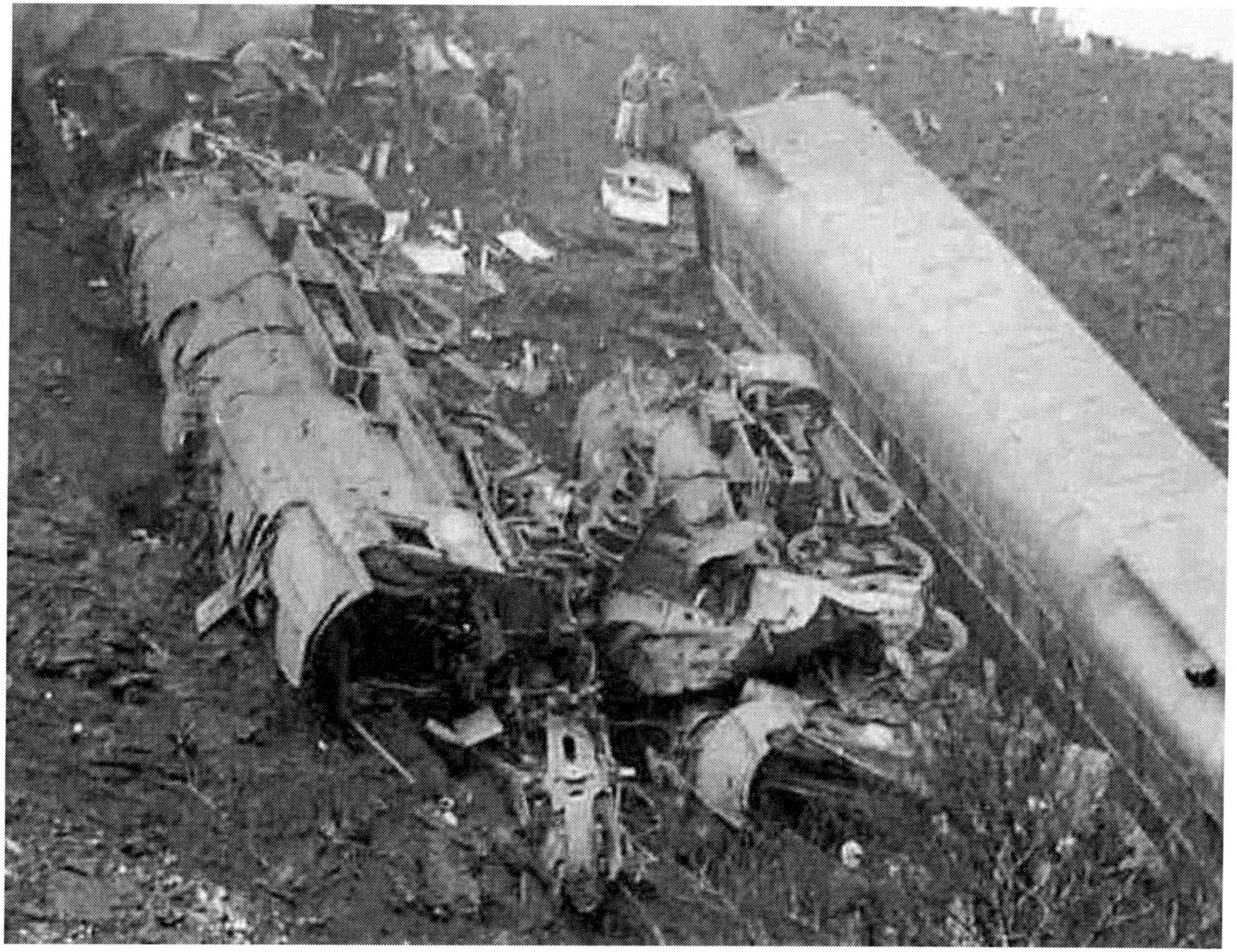

Engine 422 Engine 3771 Pullman

It was the worst possible spot and the worst possible time, 3:21 in the morning, the middle of the night. Most people were in a deep sleep and dreaming, unaware of the real-life nightmare about to unfold. The train was crowded, too; it was carrying approximately 238 passengers. Some were sitting on their suitcases. Then, breaking the silence, there was a series of loud bumps followed by the deafening sound of steel Pullman cars crashing into each other. It would be hard to figure the time that elapsed between the first seconds of derailment and the moment when everything came to rest, but to the passengers who rode it out, it must have seemed endless.

The lead engine, No. 422, and the second engine, No. 3771, came to rest on their sides next to each other. In the photo, except for the three main drive wheels, No. 3771 (in the middle) is virtually unrecognizable. Both the engineer, M.E. McCardle, and his fireman, R.K. Henry, were killed. No. 422's cab and boiler were banged up but intact. This probably helped save the life of the lead engineer, Michael S. Billig, who was banged up but intact. He was listed in critical condition with a perforated lung, chest crush injuries and steam burns. J. L. Parasock, the fireman on No. 422, was killed.

It was common to have two engines pulling together over the steep Allegheny Mountains for heavy loads. This arrangement was referred to as a "double-header." The wheel configuration for both engines was 4-6-2. That's four wheels in the front (two on each side), six driving wheels (three on each side), and one wheel on each side at the rear. The driving wheels were 80 inches in diameter.

Pennsylvania Railroad Train No. 68, the Red Arrow, was made up of two K4 engines with tenders carrying coal and water and the following cars:

1st: Baggage – mail car

2nd: Passenger baggage

3rd: Coach

4th: Sleeper

5th: Sleeper

6th: Dining

7th: Sleeper

8th: Sleeper

9th: Sleeper

10th: Sleeper

11th: Sleeper

12th: Sleeper

13th: Coach

14th: Baggage Express

The Red Arrow ran between New York and Washington and Detroit with lounge cars. From New York to Detroit it had six double bedrooms and a buffet. From Washington to Detroit it had three compartments, a drawing room, a buffet, and sleeping cars. From New York to Detroit, it had twelve sections and a drawing room, and there were three cars with ten roomettes and five double bedrooms. From Washington to Detroit and from Pittsburg to Detroit it had twelve sections and a drawing room. There were dining cars from New York to Detroit and from Washington to Harrisburg, and there were coaches from New York to Detroit and from Washington to Detroit. In earlier years, Red Arrow trains were all sleeper units.

Dining car 7960 on its left side, badly damaged

A typical dining car of the era in service

The Pennsylvania Railroad had names as well as numbers to identify its cars. Listed below are the names and numbers that made up train No. 68, the Red Arrow, as it left Pittsburgh heading east on February 18th, 1947.

Name or Class	Coupled Length	Weight of Car (lbs)
McCarr	83'-11"	174,000
Shraders	83'-11"	174,000
East Alton	83'-11"	174,000
Ogden Canyon	83'-5"	181,060
Dixieland	83'-5"	179,000
Cascade Timbers	84'-6"	125,500
Cascade Heights	84'-6"	125,500
Francis Hopkinson	82'-11"	172,100
# 5473 (mail car)	74'-4"	126,000
# 4758	77'-3"	150,000
# 4289 (coach)	79'-10"	143,700
# 7960 (diner)	81'-10"	177,500
#4013 (coach)	84'-8"	105,100
#5959 (express)	63'-10"	103,000

The following accident descriptions are taken from the
INTERSTATE COMMERCE COMMISSION REPORT
Inv. 3078

The first engine overturned to the left and stopped on its left side, down the embankment and at right angles to the tracks, 405 feet east of the point of derailment and 104 feet north of the centerline of track No. 2. The cab was demolished, steam pipes within the cab were broken and the left side of the engine was badly damaged.

The second engine overturned to the left, and stopped on its left side and against the first engine, 401 feet east of the point of derailment and 88 feet north of the centerline of track No. 2. The cab was demolished; steam pipes within the cab were broken. This engine was considered badly damaged.

The tender for each engine, carrying its coal and water, fared badly. The tender for No. 422 stopped upside down and off its trucks ('trucks' being the wheels and frame that connect to the main body); it was badly damaged. The tender for No. 3771 stopped upside down, off its trucks and badly damaged. The safety chains for both were broken.

The first car after the engines and tenders was the mail car. It stopped on its left side and down the embankment. It was considered practically demolished. Six railway mail clerks lost their lives.

The second car, passenger baggage, stopped on its left side across tracks 3 and 4. This car was considered badly damaged.

The third car, a coach, stopped with the front end on top of the first car and the rear end on track 4. The top of this car was crushed inward to the belt rail. It was considered badly damaged.

The fourth car, a sleeper car, stopped on its left side and on top of the tender of the first engine. This car was practically demolished.

The fifth car, a sleeper, stopped upright and was badly damaged.

The sixth car, a dining car, stopped on its left side down the embankment. This car was badly damaged.

The seventh car, a sleeper, stopped upright on the road bed and about 50 degrees to the tracks. This car was considerably damaged.

The eighth, ninth, and tenth cars, all sleepers, remained coupled and stopped upright across tracks

2, 3 and 4. The ninth car was the newer stainless steel model. These cars were more or less damaged.

Cars eleven, twelve, thirteen and fourteen remained upright and on track. Eleven and twelve were sleepers. Thirteen was a coach; fourteen was a baggage express. Cars eleven and thirteen were the newer stainless steel 'Budd' cars.

The division engineer said that the theoretical overturning speed for engines 422 and 3771 at the point of derailment was 65.1 miles per hour. The estimated overturning speed for the tenders, with the amount of fuel and water they were calculated to have at the time of the derailment, was 73.2 miles per hour. It appears that the train was moving at overturning speed as the engines overturned to the outside without marking the rails and slid on their left sides to the point where they stopped.

KILLED

Among the twenty-four dead were fifteen passengers, six railway mail clerks, and three train service employees, including the engineer of the second engine and the firemen of both engines.

INJURED

The engineer of the first engine and the front brakeman were both injured. The front brakeman was in the sixth car at the time of derailment. Also injured were four railway mail clerks, seven Pullman employees, four dining car employees, and 121 passengers.

The injuries ranged from life threatening to superficial, and some didn't get hurt at all.

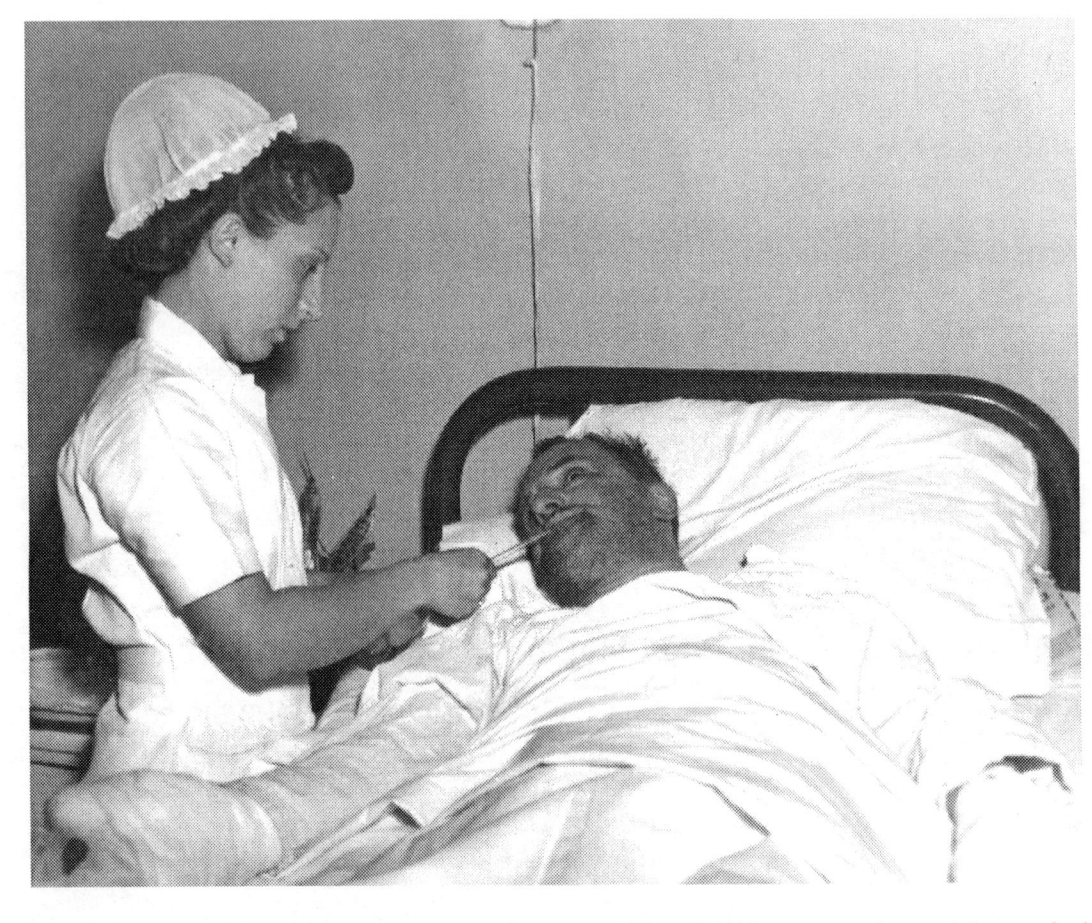

The person most likely to be killed, the lead engineer Mike Billig, wasn't. Although he sustained major injuries, including a perforated lung, chest crush injuries and burns, he survived and lived into his seventies. His daughter, Mrs. Inez Bell, a former army nurse and wife of an army doctor stationed in Puerto Rico, made a quick trip by plane and train to her father's bedside at the Altoona hospital. Both daughters, Mary and Inez, helped in their father's recovery.

ALTOONA MOBILIZED ITS
DISASTER AND EMERGENCY SERVICES WITH
SPEED AND DISPATCH

So said the ***Altoona Mirror***. The railroad station and canteen building on 12th Street was turned into a morgue, and it was soon receiving bodies brought from the crash scene by shuttle trains. Telephone operators at the city hall began coordinating information between the hospitals, undertakers and shuttle trains, and called extra doctors and nurses. The Red Cross began setting up in the station. The telephone company ran emergency lines between the station and the hospitals. It was hoped that the dead and injured list would be more accurate with communications between these two places.

Rescue crews, removing victims of the crash, and track crews, working to clear the track of the mangled wreckage, worked side by side. The Pennsylvania Railroad used all its resources to help. Crews from east and west of the scene reported for service. Coal trains crept slowly east on the two tracks that were first cleared of wreckage. Passenger trains passed in the distance over the Portage branch. Passengers from badly wrecked cars, some of which had gone over the embankment, shared the accommodations of the luckier passengers in the last seven cars that were still upright. Before sunrise, floodlights and acetylene torches lit up the night, adding to the unreal atmosphere.

The Pennsylvania State Police from the Ant Hill detail were on the scene. Six officers were on traffic duty, and fifteen assisted the Pennsylvania Railroad Police in preserving order and maintaining a guard at the scene of the accident. Eleven state policemen were on duty during the night. Special agent for the F.B.I. from the Philadelphia office, Edward A. Murphy, was making a routine investigation of the wreck in connection with espionage and sabotage possibilities. Postal inspectors were busy checking the large quantity of scattered mail. The recovered letters and packages were brought to Altoona, resorted, and forwarded to their original destinations once again. Included with the mail were several boxes of dead chicks, victims of the crash. They were stored in the Altoona post office, awaiting a claims settlement. The Public Utility Commission made an investigation of the crash, and the Interstate Commerce Commission made an in-depth report.

In an article in the **Altoona Mirror**, Conductor A. C. Gibboney said that he and his brakeman, Charles S. Kennedy, could hear cries for help as soon as they stopped their freight train, which the Red Arrow had passed moments ago. When a stop signal halted their train, they decided to walk ahead and investigate. They described their experience.

"First we heard cries for help. Then we came in range and there were people lying on the banks where they had been thrown. Some were getting to their feet and others were wandering around in a dazed condition. It was horrible in the first car, with people wedged between seats and under luggage and wreckage. Then a man, who apparently was a doctor, started to give the injured morphine pills while we gave them water to wash the pill down. It quieted them." After sending porters back to the Pullman cars for blankets, Kennedy and Gibboney went to the tool shed nearby and got hammers, hatchets and chisels to help extricate the injured. "It wasn't much to work with, but it was the best we had," Kennedy said. They made stretchers from the blankets to carry the injured back to the standing Pullmans until the arrival of the hospital train.

This photo shows how long and narrow a Pullman car really is. They were made for traveling on steel rails, made to negotiate gentle curves at modest speed — not made to tumble down steep embankments on cold winter nights.

MIDGETS, SAILORS, AND THE RUNNING MAN

Rose's Midget Revue had just finished a strenuous three-week run at the Detroit Coliseum. The Revue featured a five-piece band made up of first-rate musicians, and it included singing, dancing, and novelty acts. Some of the troupe decided to rest up during the day and take the night train to New York City. With them was Mrs. L. Rose, owner and manager of the group (referred to in the *Altoona Mirror* as being normal sized). Also taking the later train and sustaining injuries in the wreck were seven other members of the Midget Revue. Gussie Peck was the most seriously injured of the troupe, suffering a broken and lacerated left arm and a severe scalp laceration. Her sister Alice had a broken right wrist and a strained back. Jacqueline Hall had a nearly fatal experience. When the Pullman car she was riding in finally stopped its plunge, Jacqueline found herself on the bottom of a human pile. "I had three people on top of me," she said. "My girlfriend Esther Howard was on top of my head. Then there was a soldier on top of her, and my twin sister Sonja was on top of the soldier. They were all pinned down and couldn't move. I thought the weight would crush my head. Then Esther managed to crawl out, but the rest of us had to wait to be rescued."

Another seriously injured troupe member was Adelia Nowak, who had an ear almost torn off and lost a lot of blood. The ear was able to be stitched back to its normal position.

Nine sailors, who were finished with boot camp and on their way to the naval training station at Bainbridge, Maryland, spent their early morning hours pulling injured passengers out of the wreckage and administrating first aid. Later, they managed to catch the 4:40 train and returned to their base. Unfortunately, a tenth sailor suffered a fractured skull and was listed in serious condition when his buddies left for Bainbridge. All the sailors received the highest praise from the passengers for their life-saving help.

Soldiers were there to help, too. A group en route to Camp Kilmer, New Jersey gave assistance to injured passengers even as they themselves suffered. The first body that was removed from the wreck was that of Sergeant John Drumm of Dubois, Pennsylvania. The last person removed from the wreck was Sergeant Melvin Gerald Drum, also of Dubois. Similar names, same hometown, both sergeants in the army. One was killed; one survived.

Surviving wasn't easy for Sergeant Melvin Gerald Drum. He had a severely crushed right foot and leg, numerous body bruises, and head injuries. Finally, at 11 a.m., more than seven hours after the crash, rescuers were able to cut away portions of the Pullman car and extricate him. When he was finally free, Sergeant Drum was taken for a brief stay in the Altoona hospital before being taken by ambulance to the Army hospital in Carlisle, Pennsylvania.

After visiting a relative in a Pittsburgh hospital, Joseph Dutrow, age 26, found himself running down the station platform in the bitter cold to catch a train. The train he was running after was the Red Arrow, already one hour late. Joseph Dutrow didn't know it, but he was running to meet his fate. At one point in his run, he hesitated, thinking that maybe he should let this train go and catch the next one. But if he did, he would miss work the next day. He doubled his efforts and was able to jump aboard at the last minute, just before the station platform ran out. He had won the race and felt good about it.

Several hours later, as he dozed off and on, he was suddenly awakened by what felt like the coach he was riding in bouncing along the ground. In the next moment, he was flying through the air back and forth across the aisle. When all this stopped, and he was able to get his bearings, he grabbed a suitcase (he was riding in the combination baggage car and coach) and battered out some windows. Then he and a sailor set about lifting people out through the smashed windows. This was done amid people moaning, kids crying and hysterical screaming. Later, he would tell a reporter, "I wish I never caught that train. My back hurts. Look at that car. How did I ever get out alive? I haven't a scratch." No doubt the people he saved by lifting them out of coach windows were glad he didn't miss that train.

Another temptation of fate occurred when an unidentified woman and an unidentified man traded places on the train. The woman complained about feeling sick when she boarded. A male passenger gallantly offered to trade his lower berth for her upper berth. She gladly accepted. The result? She was killed in the wreck and he suffered no injuries.

The first Pullman car after the two K4 engines and their tenders was the mail car, which was staffed with ten hardworking railway mail clerks. One of these was George C. Bowman.

After surviving the initial crash, Mr. Bowman hung upside down for over eight hours while his rescuers cut away mangled steel with their acetylene torches. During those eight hours, he helped direct the rescue operation. When the postal inspector showed up, Bowman was able to identify the dead postal workers. Lastly, he made out his will on a piece of scrap paper.

When cut free, he was taken to the local hospital. He died soon after.

The photo on the following page shows three or four Pullman cars scattered on the bottom of Gum Tree Hollow.

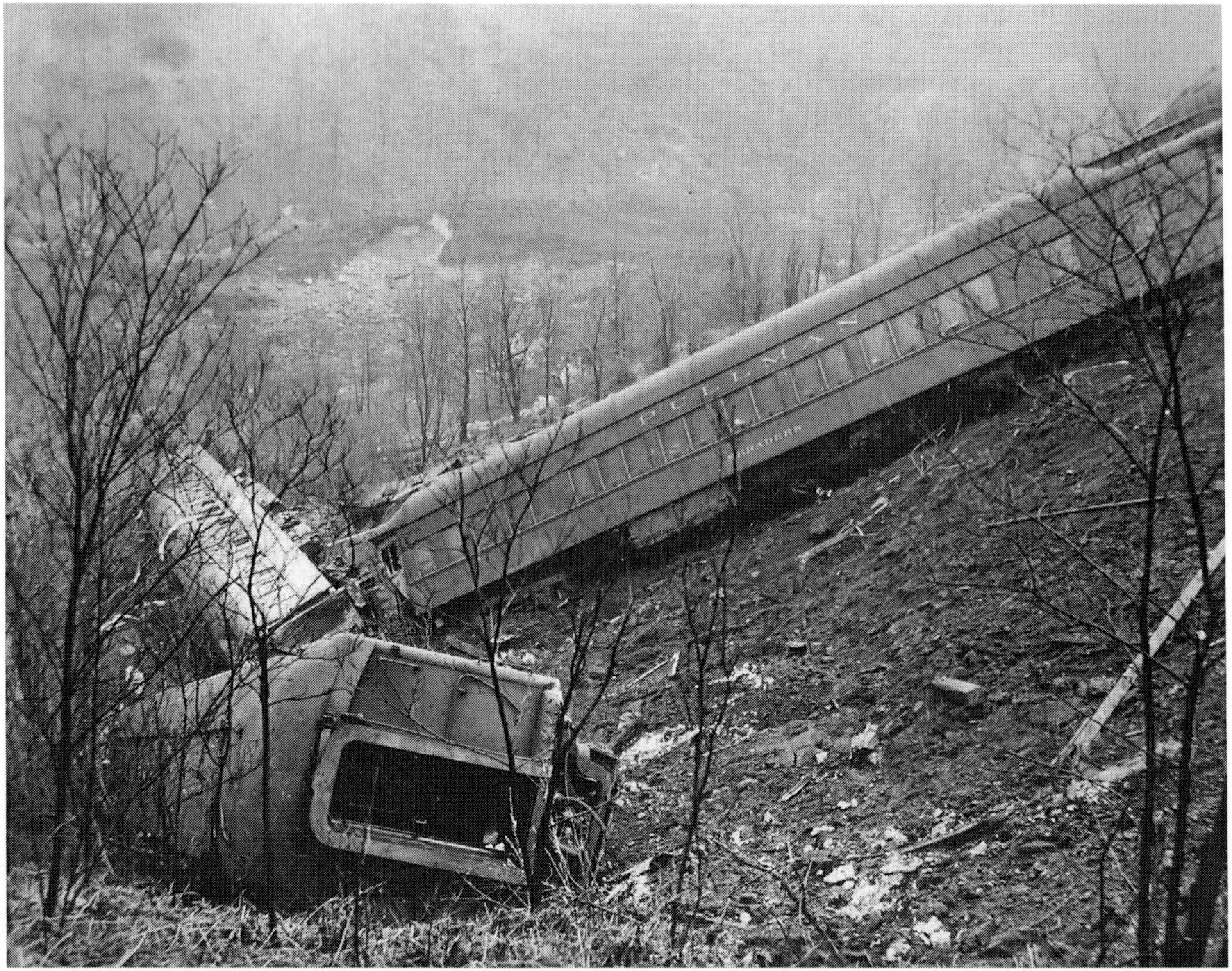

A small group of men can be seen standing in the overturned cab of engine 422

SIGHTSEEING

Well dressed sightseers

RECOVERING BODIES

The first five bodies, brought off the mountain at around 7 a.m., were placed in the baggage room behind the passenger station. At the same time, the body of a spectator who dropped dead in the station was added. The next group of dead arrived on a special train at around 12:30 p.m. The grim job of identification began under the supervision of Deputy Coroner Edgar Walls.

A number of the dead were women with little or no identification, since the bodies had been separated from their handbags in conformity with railroad regulations. This meant they had to examine each body for clothing, marks, trinkets, jewelry, birthmarks, and dentures. Most of the bodies had cinders from the railbed and embankment so badly ground into their skin that at first glance, it was hard to tell colored from white. Several were badly crushed about the head and shoulders. Several were burned with steam. The first body examined from the 12:30 p.m. hospital train was that of a boy, apparently five or six years old. His identity was not established at that time. The youth was clad in a red and blue striped jersey, blue denim trousers, and brown shoes. His body was reported to be badly mangled.

After all identifying marks were catalogued, the bodies were released to waiting undertakers. At least seven hearses were parked between the railroad tracks and the canteen building at one time, creating a somber backdrop for what was going on inside.

Earlier in the day, they had been part of the ambulance service between the station and the local hospitals. At 3 p.m., three more blanketed forms on stretchers were carried into the makeshift morgue from a rescue train. Shortly after 5 p.m., four bodies from the wrecked mail car were brought to the morgue. Several more followed during the early evening. Volunteers from the Red Cross stood by, waiting for bodies to be identified, ready to flash this information via telegram to waiting relatives throughout the east.

Miss Anna Yurkonis of Portage, a town not far from the crash site, boarded the Red Arrow in Detroit, where she worked, on her way to visit her mother in a Philadelphia hospital. She ended up in a Pullman that hurtled the lip of the embankment and landed on its side. "Everyone in our car seemed to be rolled up in a ball," she related. "For a few seconds after the crash it was quiet. Then screaming and crying broke out. Some of the passengers made flares out of rolled up newspapers and lighted them, but they were doused after fear was expressed that they might start a fire. Most of the children in the car were wrapped in bed clothing. Some of the passengers began to crawl out of the windows.

"We didn't know where we were," she continued. "It took about forty-five minutes for someone to find the roadbed of the railroad. Then we formed a chain with our hands and pulled each other up to the tracks. I had on only a dress at the time of the crash and I was really frozen by this time. I found a coat on the tracks and put it on. Some of the men went back to our car and found clothing and blankets for the children and several of the women who were slightly injured. I never did find my coat or baggage."

Some time later, a rescue train took them to Altoona. At the station, a lost five-year-old girl was reunited with her injured mother, and Miss Yurkonis boarded a train to Philadelphia.

From the collection of the
Outer Station project
Benjmin L. Bernhart.

FAMILIES

The Turek family from Altoona was on board the Red Arrow when it crashed that wintery night in 1947. All were riding in car No. 3. Most of the passengers in that coach were seriously injured. Mrs. Turek and the two girls, aged seven and four, had been visiting her parents in Detroit. Mr. Turek, a machinist for the PRR, went to Pittsburgh on Monday night and greeted his family on the train. He planned to ride with them to Altoona. At Pittsburgh, the family exchanged seats, moving from the right side of the coach to the left.

As they were nearing Altoona, both the parents and the children were dressed and ready to depart, baggage in hand. When the derailment happened, all were pinned inside the coach. Both Mr. and Mrs. Turek suffered leg injuries. The heavy winter clothing apparently helped save the two children, who had minor injuries. Mr. Turek died four days later from a punctured lung and a broken back. He was the 23rd person to die from injuries related to the crash.

A similar fate befell the Samaratani family. The two children, Raymond, nine, and Lorraine, five, plus an aunt, were uninjured. The mother, Michelina Samaratani, was killed.

The 24th and last fatality of the crash was Mrs. Ann Phillips of Detroit. She was listed as being in serious condition, and she died suddenly due to injuries sustained in the wreck. Her husband, also a patient in the hospital, was at her bedside when she died. They had been married only two days.

She was the second bride to die as a result of the wreck. Mrs. Dorothy English, whose husband was also a patient at the hospital, died a day or two after her wedding day.

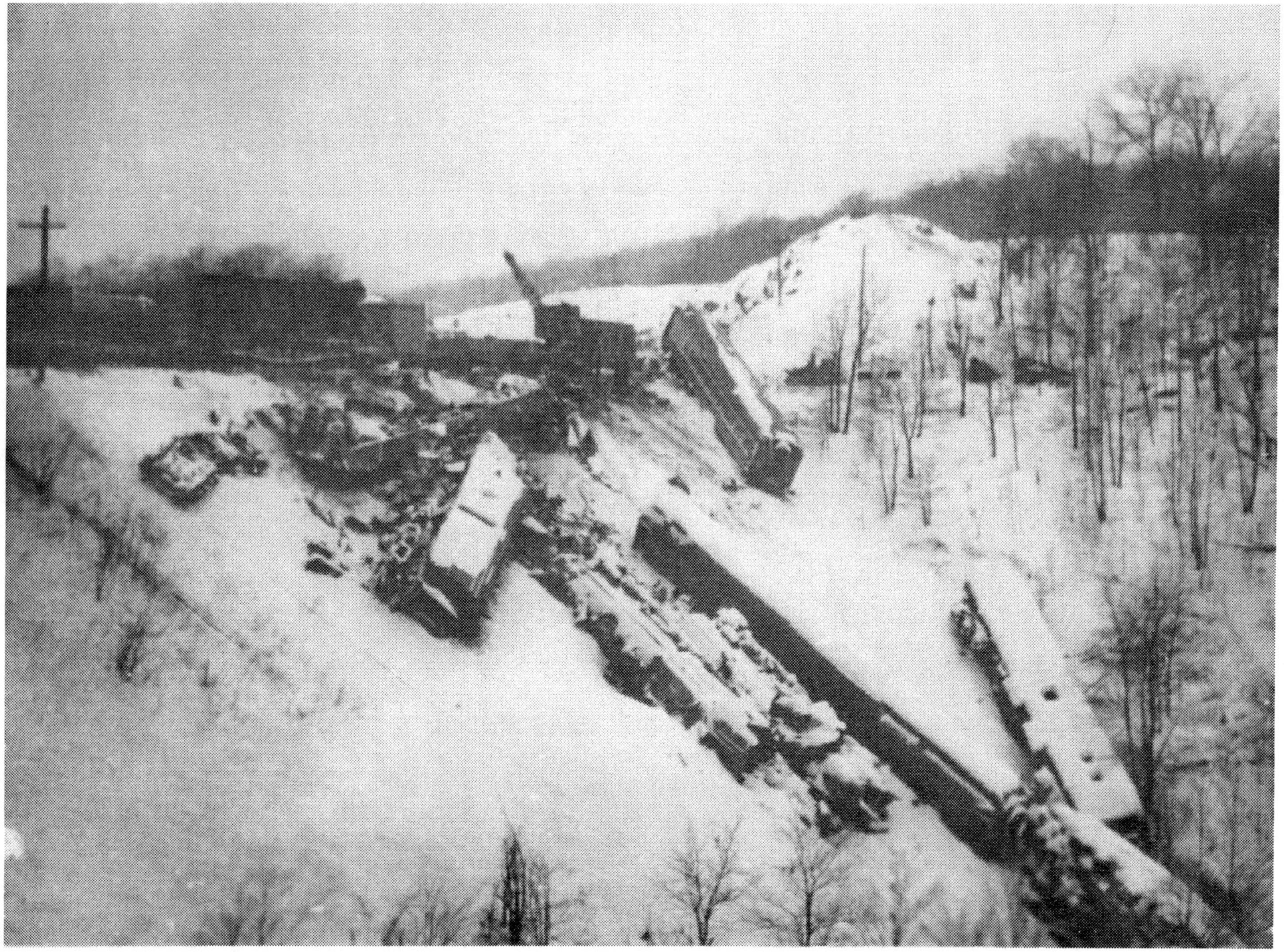

Snow at the wreck site

THE INVESTIGATION

Just how fast was the Red Arrow traveling on February 18, 1947 at 3:21 in the morning?

"Oh boy! Look at that fellow going!" a fireman on a stopped freight train, which was about a mile from the Red Arrow, testified he said as the flyer raced by. Other members of the same freight train crew put the Red Arrow's speed at forty to fifty miles per hour. The prescribed speed for Bennington Curve was thirty miles per hour. The fireman also said he thought the Red Arrow was traveling "much faster than usual." In fact, he saw sparks flying from the train's wheels as it passed, indicating the engineer was applying the brakes.

The investigation of the wreck took place in Pittsburgh on February 25. It included the Interstate Commerce Commission (page 12), the Pennsylvania Public Utilities Commerce Commission, and the Pennsylvania Railroad. Also, an on-site inspection of Bennington Curve was made while the salvage operation was in progress. Forty witnesses took part in the investigation, including two engineers, two firemen, and a rear brakeman, all from the parked freight. Mike Billig, the lead engineer, was still in the hospital in poor condition and unable to attend. The five witnesses estimated that the Red Arrow was going between thirty-five and forty-five miles per hour at a point three quarters of a mile from where the derailment occurred. Most said they saw sparks flying from the wheels.

G. R. Hershberger, conductor on the Red Arrow that night, was riding in the eighth car at the time of the crash. He testified that the train was traveling at a "slow to normal speed" on the curve. He felt the brakes being applied "now and then." Flagman Joel Bowers, riding in the thirteenth car, said, "It seemed like a normal run, the brakes worked properly when applied." Other witnesses told of examining the train before the trip and finding it in good condition.

A. J. Zimmerman, a trackman in Altoona, said he walked the Bennington Curve less than twenty-four hours before the accident and found it okay. Gullio Brandimarte, the track foreman, said he inspected the track four days before the derailment and found nothing wrong.

Photo shows a large portion of a Pullman cut away to help with rescue efforts

A BAD TWO WEEKS FOR THE PENNSY

As bad as the Red Arrow wreck was, it was just one of five accidents in less than a two-week period, three of which had fatalities. Three of the accidents occurred on the same day, two within a half hour of each other. This run of misfortune started with the Red Arrow wreck, which resulted in 24 killed and 138 injured. Ten days later, on February 28, 1947, the thirteenth and last Pullman car of the Sunshine Special, a first class passenger train bound for Texas, uncoupled. The causes of this, according to I.C.C. report #3080, were a defective coupler, defective air brakes, and a defective hand brake. The Cascade Mirage became a runaway train for more than three miles until it smashed into a outcropping of rock, just one and a quarter miles east of Bennington Curve. This happened at 4:08 a.m. The porter, Lee Keys, was crushed to death in the vestibule as he tried in vain to apply the emergency brakes. He was praised for his calmness during the wild ride.

The flagman, Edward Mulvihill, warned the passengers to lie on the aisle floor of the speeding Texas sleeper. One of the first to reach the wreck was a watchman guarding the wreckage of the Red Arrow nearby. The runaway Pullman was estimated to have been traveling at about fifty miles per hour.

Since the Cascades Mirage (all of the Pennsylvania Railroad Pullman cars had names or numbers) was the last car of the Sunshine Special, the other passengers in the first twelve cars were unaware of what had just happened. After a fifteen-minute stop at Gallitzin, they continued on their way to Texas.

On March 2, 1947, the engineer on a 48-car freight train, W. T. Dixon, was fatally crushed when his locomotive ran into the rear of a freight train standing at Kiski Junction.

On the same day, four cars of the Pennsylvania Railroad derailed and the locomotive overturned. There were no injuries.

Three cars of the Pitcairn to Altoona run derailed three miles from Bennington Curve. There were no injuries.

SIMILARITIES TO WRECKS IN THE PAST

1927: An eastbound passenger train, "The Broadway Limited," derailed near Gallitzin, PA. The lead engine came to rest on its left side. Some of the other trains were scattered and fell down an embankment, causing much damage. According to the report, the accident was caused by excessive speed.

1921: An eastbound passenger train derailed near Bennington Curve. All the coaches derailed but remained upright. The engine came to rest on its left side. The engineer and fireman were killed. Twenty passengers and one employee were injured. Just before reaching the curve, the head brakeman, Reidell, said he had a feeling that the train "would not get around it," but he was unable to explain this feeling other than to say that he had always considered it "a dangerous place."

RAISE THE RED ARROW!

Raising the wrecked Pullman cars from the bottom of Gum Tree Hollow, and the 135-ton locomotives plus their tenders from the side of the embankment, was a major engineering challenge. As a guide, the Pennsylvania Railroad was able to use a similar salvage procedure from a few years back. It involved a J1 locomotive, which is larger and heavier than a K4.

The main feature of the operation carried out by the Pittsburgh Division Workforces was to erect a tramway made up of wooden piles driven into the ground. This, in turn, would allow the locomotives to be pulled up the tramway with the help of several heavy-duty cranes. It worked.

FROM THE COLLECTION OF THE
OUTER STATION PROJECT
BENJAMIN BERNHART

This photo, taken by the author (circa 1954), shows the steel and glass concourse roof of Penn Station in New York City. Penn Station was the destination of the Red Arrow, scheduled to arrive at around 9:00 a.m. But not today. Today, it's lying in mangled pieces on a 200-foot hillside in western Pennsylvania. In about sixteen years, Penn Station itself won't be there. The steel and glass will be dismantled and carted off to the New Jersey Meadowlands to rust and corrode through the years.

In 1968, the Pennsylvania Railroad and the New York Central merged to become the Penn-Central. In 1970, the Penn-Central went bankrupt.

The newspapers of 1947 did a good job of reporting events as they unfolded at Bennington Curve. From the initial derailment to the final Pullman car recovery, the local newspapers were on top of it, and they relayed the story to the rest of the East Coast.

Now, decades later, we can relive that time by reviewing the headlines reprinted here, mistakes and all.

**City Brakeman,
Conductor Were
First on Scene**

**2 Engines, 7 Cars
Leave Track, Roll
Down 400 Feet**

25 KILLED AND 124 INJURED
IN WRECK ON P. R. R. NEAR
SCENIC HORSESHOE CURVE

**Crewmen Say
Red Arrow Speed
Was 35-45 MPH**

FIREMAN SAYS
WRECKED TRAIN
THREW SPARKS

**Probers Hear Conflict-
ing Testimony on
Red Arrow Speed at
Curve.**

140 Said Hurt In Train Wreck

"SHOCKING" QUIET OVER WRECK SCENE

CITY ORGANIZED TO ASSIST IN RAIL DISASTER

Emergency Services Respond When News of Wreck Is Received Here.

Train Wreck Victim Taken To Army Base

State Police Retain Patrol At Wreck Site

Employes Say Engines O. K.

Fatally-Injured Tyrone Man Dictates His Will Pinned In Wreckage of Red Arrow

County Doctors Treat Victims Of PRR Accident

Set Up First-Aid Station an Hour After Disaster

Minister Prays To Calm PRR Wreck Victims

Whole Family Rode Wrecked Train Tuesday

Coroner Performs Grim Task In Identifying Wreck Victims

Midgets' Rest Day Put Them on Wrecked Train

Funeral Rites Announced for Wreck Victims

REVISED LIST SHOWS DEATH TOLL NOW 22

Identification of Bodies Made Throughout Night; One Still Tentative.

Portage Woman Crawls From Wrecked Coach

PENNSY PLANS TO RAISE TWO LOCOMOTIVES

Workmen Start Building Tramway Down Slope to Pull Huge Engines to Top.

Hospital Has 25 Recovering From Wrecks

24TH VICTIM IN WRECK DIES AT HOSPITAL

ACKNOWLEDGMENTS

Altoona Mirror

Altoona Public Library

Johnstown Tribune

Railroad Museum of Pennsylvania

Railroaders Memorial Museum

Pennsylvania Railroad Technical and Historical
Society

Tunnel Museum (Gallitzin)

Clair V. Hileman

Robert Freidhoff

Margarett Greene

Tom Lynam

Robert Johnson

Berneen Finnegan

John Tomlin

Benjamin L. Bernhart

Gary Mittner

Kathryn Craft

Joseph Fogarty

Chuck Blardone

ABOUT THE AUTHOR

Born in McAdoo, PA in 1937

McAdoo High School, class of 1955

Penn State Drafting & Design, one year

40 Years Drafting in Hazleton,
Harrisburg and Philadelphia

Retired in 1999

Authored a short novel,
Strange Thunder in Jubilee

BENNINGTON CURVE

Misty and cold, the black night is shattered by a big Pennsy train that's going too fast.

The bright headlight cuts like a knife through the darkness.

It's the Red Arrow comin'…get out of the way!

This train is late and it's racing with time. The throttles wide open and the lights are all green.

Schedules are kept when you work for the Pennsy.

Out of Detroit's Fort St. Station, then east to New York as fast as you can.

Penn Station is waiting, warm and inviting, like home in the distance.

Fourteen cars pulled by two K4 engines, with their coal-laden tenders full up to the top.

Overnight travelers in eight Pullman sleepers, a dining car, mail car, coach and baggage cars, too.

Close to Altoona are the Gallitzin tunnels, and just beyond that is Bennington Curve.

It's a hard turn to the right, not meant for trains racing. Too late to slow now, too late to change fate.

In and out of the tunnel fast on track number two.

Sparks fly from wheels braking, easily seen in the night.

Now Bennington Curve is just seconds away. Full speed ahead; we're highballin' tonight.

At 3:21 derailment occurs, couplings are broken as the train jumps the track.

Like sticks in the wind the Pullmans are scattered. This way and that way, piled one on the other.

The first car, the mail car, holds six mail clerk fatalities.

Now sleeping car passengers awake to the nightmare.

The last ride for fifteen, with many more injured.

The steel giants crashing make a deafening sound, and plow up the ground beneath as they slide.

It was the pride of the fleet just moments ago. White china, white linen with black porters serving.

Everything polished and shining like new. Deluxe first class travel for people who want it.

The porters are injured, the dishes are smashed. Twisted wreckage is all to be seen.

Then all is silent, like after a battle. Hissing steam from a downed engine is all you can hear.

Where is the Red Arrow? It's long overdue. Penn Station wonders and worries some too.

Last stop tonight will be old Gum Tree Hollow.

At the bottom of Bennington curve, that's where you'll find her.

In that lonely old hollow, that dissolute place.

No crowds to greet her as she pulls in the station.

No tickets sold for a train that's not there.

It's the end of the line for a broken Red Arrow.

Now just debris on the side of a hill.

By Richard Clark